TREES & TRUTHS

Trees *and* Truths

poems by

Anntonette Jackson

628 Prince Rupert Avenue
Winnipeg, Manitoba R2K 1W2
Canada

anntonetteanna_jackson@yahoo.com

ISBN 978-1-7771946-2-8 *Paperback*
978-1-7771946-3-5 *eBook*

Contents

Acknowledgements *ix*

Dead Trees *1*
Water/Blood *2*
Poetree *3*
Puzzle Pieces *4*
The Trees *5*
Skin & Bones *7*
If I Am a Tree *8*
Contrast *9*
Trees Save Lives *10*
Exposure *11*
The Hollering Tree(s) *12*
S.O.S *13*
Trees & Truths *14*
Flesh Will Bare Trees *15*
Naked *16*
The Rose Garden *17*
The Hidden Truth *19*
Soil *20*
Faith *21*

Thousands of Ways & Seconds in Time *22*
Plenty *23*
Becoming *24*
Mirror *25*
Mind/Body/Soul *26*
Knowledge Over Power *27*
Winter Trees *28*
True Blood *29*
Black Lives Matter *30*
Silence *31*
Truth Lies Beneath Roots *32*
Law, Justice & Society *33*
Rosebud (Bonus) *34*
Wind *35*
Truth Be Told *36*
Shed/Express *37*
Skin of Lies *38*
Renew *39*
Hope *40*
Evergreens *41*
Generosity *42*
Cursive *43*
Bioluminescent Veins & Shadowed Lanes *44*
Jamaica *45*
Given Truth/Wasted Lie *46*
Summer Trees *47*
Like a Dove in the Wind *48*
The Leaves *49*
Seeds/Weeds *50*
Imagine Yourself as a Tree *51*

Truthsayer *52*
Just Like Trees *53*
Bittersweet *54*
Tree of Knowledge *55*
Seeds *56*
Trees *57*
Nature is Truth *58*
Nature's Heart Nurtures Soul (Bonus) *59*
Memory *60*
Decision *61*
Save the Trees *62*
No Truth *63*
Family Tree *64*
Trust Your Gut *65*
Forest Fire *66*
Modern Nature *67*
Autumn *68*
Beauty Never Lies *69*
Privilege *70*
Reality's Dream *71*
Grow Like a Tree *72*
Gone Tomorrow (Bonus) *73*
Echo *75*
Let There Be Light/Flowers *76*
Time *77*
Forbidden Knowledge *78*
Man Vs. Nature *79*
Plant the Truth *80*
Shadows *81*
Truth/Lies *82*

Lungs 83
Realize 84
The Roots 85
Live Laugh Love 86
A Palm Tree's Beauty 87
Truths 88
A Tree With No Leaves 89
Day & Night 90
Tree Rings & Human Fingerprints 91
The Denied Truth 92
Forest 93
True to One's Roots 94
Blue-Red (Bonus) 95
Up 97
Facts Vs. Fiction 98
Release 99
Yesterday, Today & Tomorrow 100
Branching Out 101
The Truth 102
Limbs 103
Truth & Lies 104

About the Author 107

Acknowledgements

Milena Protti: I am very grateful to have worked with Milena on my third poetry book, "Trees & Truths." I gave her the opportunity to put out her artwork for the world to observe, by including the cover art and some unique black and white illustrations of hers, for the interior of this book. I am thankful that she accepted my proposal, for this poetry book wouldn't have been achieved to the max. I found Milena on a website where people would put out their creative work; I was looking for someone who could do art covers for poetry books, I happened to come across Milena and I do not regret running into her 'til this day. Milena is such an inspiration; she inspired me to keep on writing poetry, while she would never give up painting. We support one another, by sharing our thoughts and views on one another's art. I am owing her a million thanks, though I wish I could give her a million hugs as well. (Milena's Instagram: *@theartsymile*).

Mother Nature: I want to dedicate this book to the trees, for aiding me to connect with nature more than I ever had a long time ago. I learnt to become calm and at peace with Mother Nature when she is blowing a storm my way. As I was writing "Trees & Truths," I found that trees are no different from us, that they have the same features as humans, from the beginning of time. I remember when I was little, I would be afraid of storms turning into tornadoes, then as I grew, I learnt that tornadoes do not pass-through cities; I sleep through thunderstorms knowing Mother Nature is just going through a phase, like how we too have our moods. (Dedicated to the trees who have found their truth, and to their roots that grew knotted, encrypted with knowledge).

Lastly, I would like to thank John van der Woude for publishing/designing *Trees & Truths*. Without John, this book wouldn't have made it on Amazon. (John's Email/ Website: *john@jvdwdesigns.com*, *jvdwdesigns.com*).

Thank you very much,
and I hope whoever is reading, enjoys this book.

Dead Trees

There are trees that have died.
Where apples can't bear onto anymore,
where leaves are forced to pluck themselves off of.
We are like dead trees—still holding onto parts of ourselves,
leaving the other segments for our descendants to trace.

- *Trees that die, still have at least some life they carry.*

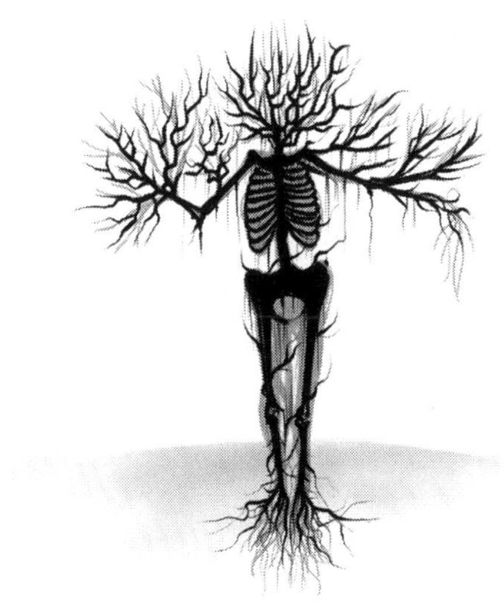

Water/Blood

There is a reason why water is pure,
and blood is crimson,
for it would be far too deep to dive for our truths below sea level,
and far too painful to try and bring to light the lies in our veins.

- *Blood is thicker than water; you'll drown quicker in a lie than you ever would telling the truth.*

Poetree

Trees are poems earth jots across valleys;
while we turn them into paper,
nature becomes the ink
that may take note of our emptiness.

- *Buds are the rough drafts in which trees master their poetry from, becoming the art of nature.*

Puzzle Pieces

The truth is like jigsaw puzzles
composed of many parts,
that fit to form a picture,
a masterpiece of art.
When a piece doesn't fit
in order to disguise,
no longer will we have the truth,
but only a patch of lies.

- *Take things all apart, and put them back together again. (A masterpiece in the flesh)*

The Trees

With the summer night's breeze
and the pouring rain,
the trees whispers their truths
with each LEAF,
as nature breathes green.

With the summer night's moon
and glistening stars,
the trees plant their dreams
with each SEED,
as nature appears serene.

With the summer morning's sky
and the fluffy clouds,
the trees stretch their limbs
with each BRANCH,
as nature runs in between.

...

With the summer morning's sun
and boiling heat,
the trees mark their souls
with each ROOT,
as nature becomes keen.

- *Each leaf, seed, branch, and root makes*
  a tree, its own unique being.

Skin & Bones

Don't be like those bones that hide under skins,
because eventually your flesh will start to decay,
revealing fractured joints with aches and sins.
You should always be bare;
like the truth, as the clay—naked to the point where your
soul is white, almost pure.

Never be the skin that cover up bones,
because the lies will begin to sink in between tissues,
breaking broken muscles like sticks and stones.
You are also rare; like gold, with hidden issues
where your body grows old, a living cure.

- *Form of emptiness is the zone of possibility that exists between skin and bone.*

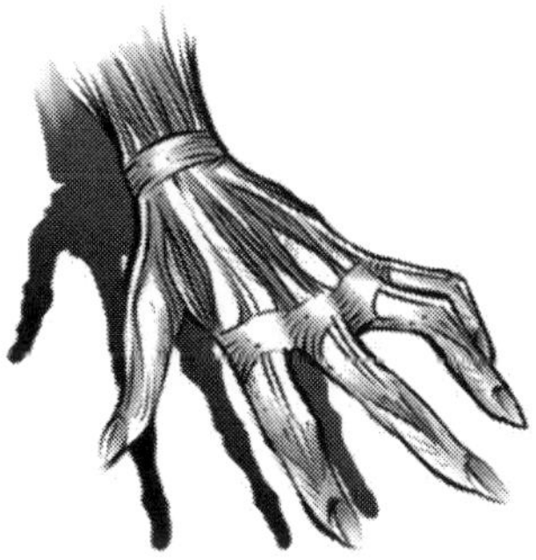

If I Am a Tree

If I am a tree,
I want you to be the wind
that astounds me
with every move.

If I am a tree,
I want you to be the rain
that waters me
through the dry season.

If I am a tree,
I want you to be the sun
that strengthens me
by the shine of light.

- *The trees around me, made me believe that I am not a human being anymore, but a tree amongst them.*

Contrast

We found ourselves beaming around light
while they got lost wandering in the dark.

The sun was down
when welcomed them our lives.
The moon was up
when we told them our goodbyes.

We told the truth
to the point where things got hard for us.
They spat their lies
to the point where life got easier for them.

- *Life's highest bliss only exists in polarity*
  with the deepest sadness and regrets.

Trees Save Lives

How ~~familiar~~ similar are you with trees?
Your marks, your scars from your skin is mirrored by a tree's
bark.
So remember if you ever wanted to axe down a tree,
you would be creating more bruises
to your own familiar body.

Why can't you ~~burn~~ take advantage of trees?
Their seeds, their soils from their roots are productive
that they never stop to supply oxygen.
So remember if you ever wanted to light a tree on fire,
you would cause the air you breathe
to burn your own lungs.

- *Seize the axe from those who don't ask.*

Exposure

Our truths will bounce back
like the television light
in complete dark,

exposing ourselves from shadows
that lurk upon white walls
as some kind of lie,

we might as well confess
towards our wrongful sins
than suffer through the void.

- *We found our truths in dangerous places
they warned us not to go in.*

The Hollering Tree(s)

As trees scream,
the wind howled with them.
When the trees chant for eternity
animals listen to their songs,
protecting those forests—guarding these woods.
But while a single tree calls out man's name
he doesn't hear the cries,
burning the leaves—chopping down trunks.

- *We are so deafened by our own society that we aren't aware of what Mother Nature needs, when she calls to us.*

S.O.S

The truth begins to sink in
like a broken ship lost at sea,
shipwrecked to the core.

We find ourselves drowning in our own tears,
reaching for comfort,
each breath becomes more painful
as we swim to shore.

- *The truth may cause us pain, before giving us a new realm to freedom.*

Trees & Truths

If we'd appreciate the trees
we will see the truth,
we could let the lies fall to the ground
leaving fresh leaves on branches,
then the light can reach the roots.

- *Shedding the lies around us like dead leaves and not only starting afresh through budding innocence (new leaves), but also allowing the nurturing roots of innocence to be "open", to clear the light of day—representing the future growth of truth.*

Flesh Will Bare Trees

Make nests of hair
and boughs of arms,
sow seeds in palms
as nude branches tear.

Like barks leave scars
from trunks of brown,
as a tree takes crown
plants shot like stars.

If wombs unveil no fruit
then flesh will bare trees,
approved by all new leaves
we will become ancient root.

- *These trees still bare strange fruits, that sometimes cannot be eaten by man.*

Naked

I think that our bodies are naked in truth.
We are only gently covered with button clothing;
and beneath these garments are skin, bones and silence.

- *Some people reach inside themselves to learn
the greater unknown, still others crawl inside
their shells not wanting to be shown.*

The Rose Garden

I will never forget how seeds led me close to my comfort home;
seeds that were rooted beneath the rose garden—
    a place I could call my own,
where plants shot up from each seed like a welcomed
    house guest
as I watered every single one
of these visitors;
some turn up as awful weeds
that would try and destroy my garden,
others bloom as colourful flowers
that can paint their beautiful presence;
the weeds are no longer allowed
in my garden full to be flourished,
while roses brought warm greetings to these grounds
become much more like relatives;
I don't remember being this close to comfort
within a garden like this,
when the seeds showed me my past
underneath the soil as I plant my future fields;
soil that held plants named in my native tongue,
though I do not pardon
the grasping roots of foreign bushes intruding in my garden;

...

instead I will carve them
into my own shrubs,
where seeds can sprout
from this natural womb I call land.

- *The earth is your garden in which you remove weeds of doubt and replace them with seeds of hope.*

The Hidden Truth

To discover the undiscovered
deep discarded truth,
is to leave behind the covered
betrayals of our youth.

- *A youth who covers up their lies, is like walking around with a bloody knife in their hands; stabbing at the truth until the truth bleeds out, leaving lies as old bloodstains.*

Soil

The trees that watch as I write
would sway with the breeze
as if all that blends
underneath the soil is a little spark of knowledge
where roots will peek through and push past,
towards the light.

- *How do the roots know, they must climb towards light but stay intact with their soil?*

Faith

One of the foundations of having faith in ourselves,
is to actually face the truth of our very own imperfections.

- *Stay true to yourself.*

Thousands of Ways & Seconds in Time

As though there were a thousand ways,
wrapped in splendid sunlight
was a way to be seen.
With such weary skies—the trees stand tall with worry,
withering in the wind of tomorrow.
They thought of us as strong survivors,
but instead we were suffocating—until the trees sacrificed
their seconds in time.

- *We're breathing but then we're not, but it's okay because we're hugging the trees.*

Plenty

So many unknown
truths.
Untold
lies.
People struggle and lose
themselves in disguise.

Too much rotten
perfections.
Hidden
flaws.
People maintain and find
themselves within the cause.

- *Only silence now; contains our bitter truths.*

Becoming

Our hands clung tightly on branches.
Our arms begin to become those branches.
From the trees that gave us strength to surround.

Our skin turns to bark—as the wind blows.
Our bodies begin to form small hollows,
in the center of our tummies.
From the bark that once was lost but now found.

The hair on our heads turn to leaves—as it rains.
Our roots begin to grow fresh fruits,
out of our scalps.
Apart from the old leaves that fell to the ground.

- *It is when we become the trees,*
  we will start to know ourselves
  and have a sense of belonging.

Mirror

The lies will shatter
bringing shards of glass with it.

Reflections will not end
from a broken mirror.

Our images will reveal
the truth through pain.

- *Sometimes we have to shatter the mirror within us,*
  to see all of the pieces that makes us beautiful.

Mind/Body/Soul

Let your mind find its place to grow,
as a tree finds its place in the snow.

Let your body straighten after the pain,
as a tree straightens after the rain.

Let your soul hold on while it forms,
as a tree holds on while it storms.

- *What good was it to feel a body, when we could rest inside our souls?*

Knowledge Over Power

In order to tell the truth,
we do not need to have power over others.
Power is something we only need in order to spread lies,
to mouth empty words and pretend they are true.

- *Hold your knowledge over power, it will get you by when telling what is true from false.*

Winter Trees

The naked trees
when winter disappears,
gradually cover their bare bodies
with green garments.

The harsh winter
cannot claim victory
until the last leaf falls
from naked trees.

- *In the winter, do leaves live in hiding with the roots?*

True Blood

When the truth spills,
the blood begins to regain its pigment
bring oxygen in motion.
Whenever we tell a lie,
our heart begins to divide in segments
casting shadows in between each portion.

- *Carry the truth within your heart, for it will set the heart ablaze.*

Black Lives Matter

You watched our African ancestors
get whipped until the skin on their backs
resembled the bark on trees.

You witnessed black people
get hung from trees,
until their blood flooded the leaves.

- *The tree against the strong gust;*
  bend in protest to keep from falling,
  like people of color against racism;
  shout in rallies to keep from being killed.

Silence

Sometimes staying silent
wins the argument.

Sometimes keeping quiet
avoids the drama.

Sometimes ignoring them
stops the conflict.

But most of the time,
silence is violence.

- *Silences, makes more noise than the truth.*

Truth Lies Beneath Roots

A gust of air
startles August trees,
to part each leaf off their limbs;
while the gentle breeze
whispers into their hollows,
to tell them, they are never alone.
— Wind

A splash of water
drowns spring flowers,
to weaken each one of their petals;
while the steady drizzle
sprinkles down within their soils,
to remind them, they can flourish again.
— Rain

A spark of flame
burns night's forest,
to destroy each of their fruits;
while the blazing sun
shines light through their spirits,
to show them, they're more than just darkness.
— Fire

Law, Justice & Society

If truth is the law,
they have no case
they're just a waste
of time and space.

If truth is justice,
they have no rights
they're just some heist
that started the fights.

If truth is society,
they have no lives
they're just the lies
stabbed by knives.

- *Nothing terrifies the truth.*

Rosebud (Bonus)

Rose petals scattered in red,
around their entire flowerbed.
As if the wind blew away each stain,
for that one rose to heal once again.
The wind began to speak to this rose,
with a whistle from beneath the shadows.
With light wind comes steady rain,
where new petals for rose will sustain.
This new flower will stand out from those,
may Mother Earth see how it grows.
Rose stems join together in wed
around the sunlight that began to shed.

- *The rosebud that always promises a new life between the ones who are ready at the end of their lifetimes, they know when their legacy will live on. A single rose and yet we know, in our hearts it will blossom, wither and die. Hope and faith tell us yet another rose—linked in ways our minds cannot comprehend, will bud anew. So we look forward, beyond thorns and dried petals to life.*

Wind

Although wind whistled through the trees,
there was more stillness in the air.

Although wind blew away the leaves,
there was more room on the branches.

- *Let the wind caress every part of one's soul.*

Truth Be Told

True words that they've kept silent
deep within their throats,
lingering inside their mouths,
and hanging from the tip of their tongues;
are beginning to transform into false sentences
mashed up inside their minds,
confusing to each of their brain cells.

- *True words became false sentences, as false sentences became lying paragraphs; these paragraphs are murmured as stories, but we should know that whispered sentences aren't truths, only clear words that are heard and spoken.*

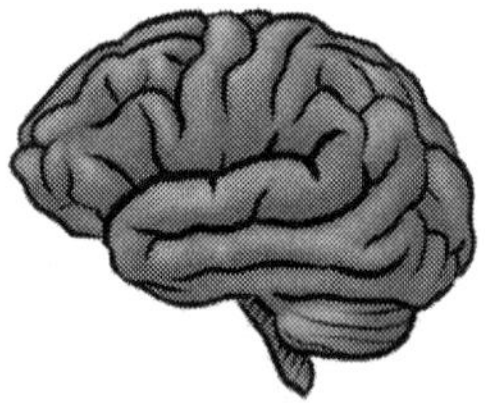

Shed/Express

The trees,
saw us shedding our tears
and now
they are shedding their leaves.

The trees,
saw us expressing our peacefulness
and now
they are expressing their stillness.

- *Trees also have feelings.*

Skin of Lies

The skin of lies will burn
when we touch the light
and allow our souls
to become submerged in truth.

But even death can't destroy the truth
destined to resurface,
due to our souls living on,
and the skin of lies decaying.

- *Even truth has been stripped of its flesh.*

Renew

We all felt ourselves sink into the trees' surface,
feeling our loneliness swept away by wilderness.
Where we lost a part of our energy that society drained,
but encountered all of sunlight that nature supplied.

- *Our hearts would have been a forest mixed*
  with variety of trees, if our souls were filled with
  wilderness. So let our souls get lost in the wilderness,
  to fill our voided hearts from emptiness.

Hope

Far from our pain,
comes a grain of truths in every lie;
and within our bodies lies the truth of our eternal sins;
captured in a jar that would remain
until the end of our days,
when feelings and raw emotions unfold
and all of humanity consumes the battle of truths.
That far outweigh these lies,
Leaving the world with a little hope.

- *Fight for the truth in hope you will survive.*

Evergreens

Climb to the top of my tree,
bend the branches of wire,
and let me wrap you
in the paper of evergreens.

- *Surround yourself with trees and bond with them; as they grow, so will you.*

Generosity

A greed for the truth
Goes hidden
Inside a heart that pleads.

Our offerings
Will strengthen
For borrows that give.

Agreed to satisfaction
Each within
Our kind hearts that share.

- *Sometimes we can afford to lose a lot for the lies we tell, just because we cannot let the truth be free. So what if honesty costs more than you can afford to lose?*

Cursive

We cannot seem to decipher,
the trees scribbled in cursive roots.

Only our own cursive handwriting,
we can seem to decode.

- *Trees seem to send messages down to their roots, that they can only understand.*

Bioluminescent Veins & Shadowed Lanes

Some people's words are fragile veins, bioluminescent
and blue.
Too delicate for the truth
they try to find,
very sensitive about their pain
they never seem to hide.

Some people's words are hidden lanes,
shadowed and black.
Too dark for the lies
they never seem to find,
very secretive about their nightmares
they try to hide.

- *Our veins bursting is like when a tree's branch snaps. We begin to lose a part ourselves, but gain something from the pain.*

Jamaica

This island paints herself with foreign trees.
Where walking barefooted on grass
without the use of her dialect is a fault.
A tropical region,
where earth's breath is still visible,
and where hills still express their meaning.
The palm trees and exotic fruits command this island now,
where Jamaican patois
is driven within roots.

- *Jamaica, the land of wood and water.*

Given Truth/Wasted Lie

Give me the truth of you,
whether stitched together
or broken in thousand pieces
waiting to be built anew.

Discard the lies inside of you,
whether it's keeping you sane
or driven you over the edge
where death will be due.

- *Truths, hidden in mythical depths.*
  Secrets, revealed in life's last breaths.

Summer Trees

Trees stand hot
in the sun,
just to keep us cool
in their shade.

- *The summer days grow hotter,*
  as the summer nights grow cooler.

Like a Dove in the Wind

My heart flutters,
like a winged-dove flying through the air.
My blood cells are firstly coated in red,
warmth...
Then elegantly dressed in white,
purity...
The truth comes intact with my soul
and sets me free,
like doves in the wind.

- *Watch how doves scatter their truths freely across the horizon. We must pour our souls into the truth or it will become voided with lies.*

The Leaves

Not only do leaves change color,
their texture is different from the tree;
A masked identity.
The tree will shed those leaves to the ground,
a wise move—to rid negativity.
These leaves wish they were roots,
because roots never leave a tree.

- *Most of society only sees what's on the surface (leaves). You only see the outside, but we must learn to decipher all of that, and actually see what's on the inside of a person (roots).*

Seeds/Weeds

Truths are deepened
as the seeds.

Lies are weakened
like the weeds.

- *We must pluck the weeds (lies), from the seeds (truths) that feed them. If left unchecked, the lies will multiply until the field is overrun by weeds, leaving the truth (seeds) hidden.*

Imagine Yourself as a Tree

Imagine yourself as a tree,
moving from field to field
planted by weather or will.
No need to pretend that dying is easy—plants have
  withered before you.
So whether you wish to stay or dismantle through,
allow yourself to settle into the soil
knowing the earth is no man's
but the roots are yours.

- *A tree's root goes buried in its traditional soil.*

Truthsayer

You are the truthsayer,
with light and an held torch.
Speak with your tongue,
as if it were on fire.
Don't let censored words
put out the spark,
nor the false gags
muffle your voice.

- *Do you swear to the tell the truth, the whole truth, and nothing but the truth?*

Just Like Trees

The same way a tree feels its dead leaves departing
    from its limbs,
we feel old friends slipping out of our lives;
Just like the tree won't lose hope over old feelings
    to new beginnings.
We know that just like trees
have more room for stronger roots to grow,
we can have space to build new friends.

- *A tree might happen to become your friend.*

Bittersweet

Truths like fresh lemon
dangling on an old citrus tree;
Waiting to be picked.
While those unwanted lies
become rotten oranges,
that fell uneaten from branches to soil.

- *Nibble on the truth, no matter how bitter it may taste.*

Tree of Knowledge

They teared off the forbidden fruit
from the tree of knowledge
without nature's consent.

- *The knowledge they don't acknowledge.*

Seeds

They tried to tear out our roots,
and burn us like weeds.
But they didn't see our fruits,
never knew we were the seeds.

- *Can't kill the truth.*

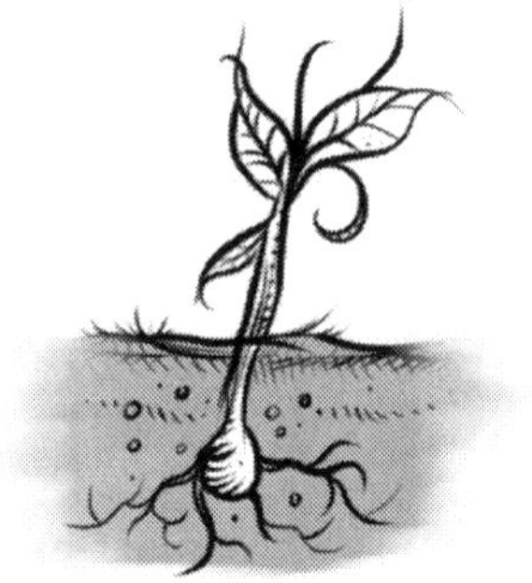

Trees

Trees stand tall
Endure stormy weathers

Trees don't fall in despair
When they are bare

Trees dance
to the wind's song.

Trees are generous
They offer fruit and roses

- *There are ways to count the trees before they fall.*

Nature is Truth

Nature was peaceful,
until man built his corruption
upon the land
that ancient trees once claimed.

Society is lost,
with the truth being suffocated
by the pollution
we spread across the air we breathe.

- *Nature is truth, disturbed by fictions we prefer.*

Nature's Heart Nurtures Soul (Bonus)

Blue is the hue to our sorrows
that weeps,
sinking in tears under the warm sunset
Rain is the pattern for the sparrows
that flies,
finding which way to soar when wet.

Pink is the shade to a heart
that heals,
guiding love through the blood
Peony is a flower within art
that blooms,
maturing its petals from bud.

- *Green is the color of trees and plants that sprout up in June. Blue and red; Memories of love and happiness but also pain and sadness are visible in two of these pairs. Swimming in patches of light. Images become blurry from the tears that pour from a broken heart. Sparrows follow the direction of sunsets, leaving the harsh winter to nest.*

Memory

As forgotten memories pass by like shadows of the
trees over dead grass,
old leaves seem to be made almost entirely out of
memory—making them alive again,
with the wind.

- *The sense of amnesia is like a forest being burned alive; a traumatic event where a tree will become residue and not knowing where its ashes will end up to, when it tries to plant itself again.*

Decision

A decision
came to me
like lightning,
and it struck itself
in branches
deep within the root
towards my truth.

The truth
took a solid turn
for roots
that made branches,
securing me
from the pain
while I made
my decision.

- *Decide on what's real. Be open to the change. Release yourself from your own prison. Because not making a decision, is still a decision.*

Save the Trees

The seeds and plants begin renewal's churn,
producing leaves and roots for which we yearn.
But the trees we continue to burn,
will shrivel up and may never return.

- *If it weren't for the trees, how would we breathe?*

No Truth

For there is no truth, no honor, no relief,
no real understanding, no trust or belief.
We eat without tasting, we rest without sun,
We drink without thirst, we laugh with no fun.
We sing with no tune, we speak with no thought,
And lie to ourselves from what we were taught.

- *What's a world with no truth?*

Family Tree

We dived deep within our beings,
and sought to decrypt the timeless data encrypted in the branches of our DNA
to extract the juice of the fruit
from the tree of life,
and paint our family's name
like scars embedded upon tree trunks.

- *Most trees carried the* DNA *of our ancestors' bones.*

Trust Your Gut

We thought of lying,
kept it deep within our brains
until we imagined fake 'scenarios'
inside our heads.

We swallowed the truth,
hid it deep inside our stomachs
until we encountered that butterfly 'feeling'
within our tummies.

- *We should always trust our gut,*
  not lies we build up in our minds.

Forest Fire

The tree watched...
as all it knows it will become ash
waving goodbye in the wind.
A leaf ushers the smoke
to its new place in the sky;
leaves will turn into the ash of memory
from that burned down tree.

- *The whim of wind and seed set the fate of every leaf and tree.*

Modern Nature

One nature—a lifesaver,
to many species looking for a way out, towards freedom.
The light—a white savior,
to ones who hid their truth in the dark,
for too long.

- *Mankind seems like failure. To feel that we've succeeded, we must look to nature without damaging it.*

Autumn

It's that time of season
where we welcome autumnal leaves
and say goodbye to emerald trees.

It's that time to reason
with nature changes along the breeze
and to feel the continuous days with ease.

- *There's a time in autumn when the trees change their nature, and wake up beyond matter; then we see them come back to their original selves.*

Beauty Never Lies

If they can't see that genuine smile of ours,
we'll just have to rely on our eyes for beauty.

- *Our eyes will always tell the honest truth, even if we try and fake a smile beneath falsity.*

Privilege

The root of the problem,
is to go through the branches;
There you will find light
reflecting off each leaf,
a chance for the tree
to let go and set leaves free.

- *To enlighten a tree, the leaves no longer need.*

Reality's Dream

Don't let your dreams tell lies
let them show you what they know,
they see through inner eyes
so don't try to gain control.

Waking up is harder on you,
when dreaming is all you seem to do.

- *Identify truths in reality through your own observations.*

Grow Like a Tree

I wish to grow like a tree,
to keep the past deep inside of me,
to let my roots adjust,
as I stand tall against the gust.

- *We are the trees, that our ancestors planted.*

Gone Tomorrow (Bonus)

I know your thoughts are hard to express,
when your heart is filled with tenderness.
But how would you feel the sorrow,
if your love was gone tomorrow?
Would you turn to death's door
knowing love is all done for?
It would be no use to die,
without use of goodbye.
As you waited too long,
your love is now gone.
Time has passed you,
love cannot be true.
What is tomorrow,
without sorrow?
Try expressing,
your blessing.
Never hate,
appreciate.

- *Love is becoming harder to express, but easy to encounter the emotions in our hearts. We are afraid that when time passes by, it's harder to face the truth in love. True love with another will vanish, if we don't reveal our feelings on time. If we begin to show hatred because love is hard to explain; Tomorrow we will run into sorrow and regret, if a little love isn't shown today.*

Echo

Heard shallow voices
from the ancient woods today,
echoing out the hollow of trees;
The wind tried to escape their cavity,
but air was trapped in
as the murmurs crawled out.
We couldn't hear
the breeze blowing in our ears,
due to the screaming
echoes of their fears.
It was the trees' own echo
that had enough of these woods,
shouting for us to plant new forests.

- *Lost in the woods? Follow the tree's path, listen to the forest's echo.*

Let There Be Light/Flowers

Ignite the truth and let it burn,
so the light can emerge
from the lies that was once dim.

Water the trees and let them grow,
so the flowers can bloom
from the leaves that were once dry.

- *Ignite the truth, not innocent trees.*

Time

A tree—Our present
Buried roots—Our past
Leaves blowing off the branch—Our future

- *Time will tell, a tree's farewell.*

Forbidden Knowledge

And yet the various priesthoods hint that all the toil,
pain and death itself came down on humanity,
all because a woman nibbled at forbidden knowledge
known as the "hidden" truth...
The art could very well be the pair in the garden East
of Eden.

- *Forbidden Knowledge can destroy mankind, but it can never eat away nature (Nature always restores itself).*

Man Vs. Nature

Mankind axed down that tree
tore off its remaining leaves
chewed up the ripened fruits
and left the roots to rot in dirt.

- *Mother Nature is very disappointed in mankind.*

Plant the Truth

The truth is not made up in words or even deeds;
It is far too subtle to be seen or heard.
It's in a garden that nurtures our needs,
too diverse for any act or word.

The truth is made up of plants and flowers;
it will grow with no use of evil or powers.
It is deep within the root of our palms,
too good for any chaos or bombs.

- *So plant the truth rather more than speak it, because it will carry thorns that may cut our throats.*

Shadows

A tree endures darkness every night,
knowing the sun will come out eventually.
So, we too, must learn to embrace
our shadows within
so that we can understand
what it really means to grow.

- *Look up at the sky at night, you will see the trees baring in the dark.*

Truth/Lies

Lies are woven,
masks are made.

Truths are hidden,
lives may fade.

- *Lies, in a sense, are something we wear—they mask, make us seem like something we're not—in that sense they're unnatural, fake. Our natural and true state—going back to the Garden of Eden (when we loved the trees) is truth.*

Lungs

Earth.
We have ruined the Earth.
Pollution reigns in the air and seeps into our lungs.
We welcome it into our lungs as if it was a guest.
But it's not. It's the enemy that contaminates our oxygen.
The oxygen released by trees.
We have ruined the tree's effort,
in keeping us to breathe.

- *Absorbing sun's caring embrace and the water's surge of purification, the trees mix them into oxygen for the man, and what did man did in return for the trees?*

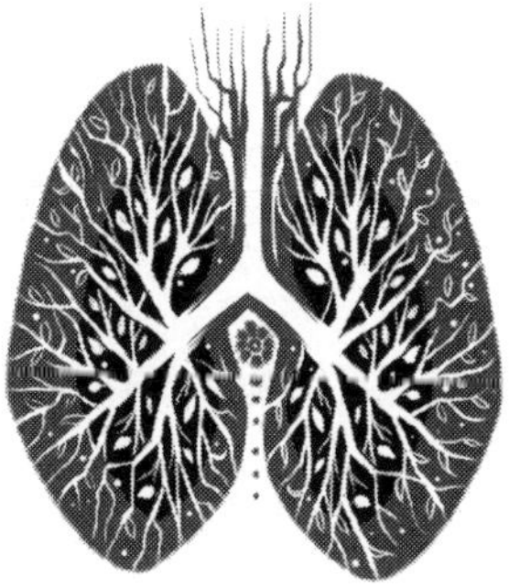

Realize

Realization of the truth
is nothing less than magic
it eliminates regrets,
fears and takes away everything tragic.

- *Realizing the truth can release so much pressure off of us, from lies we carry as burden.*

The Roots

Unlike leaves,
roots are always a part of trees,
they stay the same, keeping the tree alive—
almost sane.
The roots tell the tree's true story,
we just have to dig deep to listen.

- *If you actually want to know the truth, you can't find it above surface level, we cannot only admire leaves. You have to look below the dirt. Hence, finding roots.*

Live Laugh Love

Dear Truth,
we live to laugh
we live to love
our lives are like true colors
living on a painter's canvas.

Dear Wisdom,
we laugh to live
we laugh to love
our laughs are of wise people
laughing away when anxious.

Dear Knowledge,
we love to live
we love to laugh
our desires are the acknowledgement
loving ourselves through happiness.

- *It's easier to tell lies through words. Show love by expressing the truth through your actions, that way your heart is doing the talking instead of your mouth.*

A Palm Tree's Beauty

Tall as a palm tree
strong compared to its roots
hair natural like the leaves
complexion alike rich soils
stretch marks resembling bark.

- *Bear the marks, the evidence that not only have we lived, but the strength from our roots brought forth new life, existing as whole; Just like a palm tree still stands.*

Truths

Some truths are harder to face
and difficult to speak out.
But when we let them sprout
the burden on our hearts will erase.

- *Don't be afraid to speak the truth.*

A Tree With No Leaves

A tree with no leaves,
can tell us many stories.

If we listen to the wind,
we can hear the leaves
that used to exist on that very tree.

A tree with no leaves,
has many mysteries.

If we touch the sap in a tree,
we will have the feel
of tree's blood on our hands.

A tree with no leaves,
is just as alive as a tree with leaves.

- *For those who can't hear the leaves, must sense the trees.*

Day & Night

The daylight reveals the truth after all
Until the night when darkness falls.

- *Truth is dawning; a day break.*

Tree Rings & Human Fingerprints

Tree rings go buried
within its stump,
as do the fingerprints
that run deep
within our skin.

- *Trees evolve around/inside of us.*

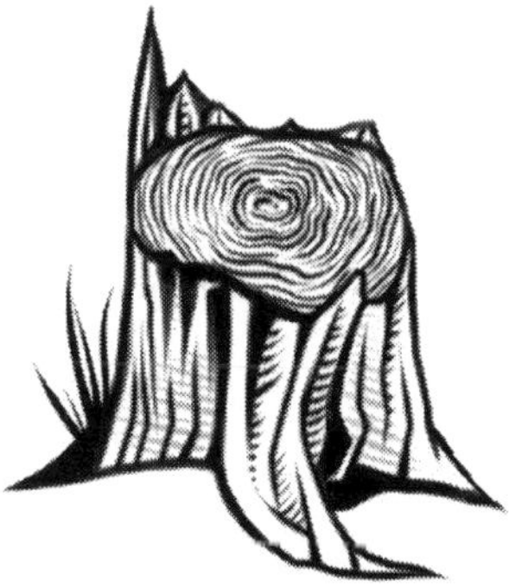

The Denied Truth

Denied truth
is the forbidden fruit,
it is harder to resist
and catches us in the end
once eaten.

- *We will not get very far if we try to escape the truth, we are carrying within us. The denied truth will be with us wherever we flee.*

Forest

You never feel so much
growth.
Until a day,
when you take a long walk
through the forest
and come out
wiser than the trees.

- *Some people are like trees, growing up strong mentally from getting enlightened, making them get wiser (taller) as they grow.*

True to One's Roots

I've never been that type of woman who hid her truth
beneath the dirt,
or fake a smile beneath the hurt.

I've been the type of woman who admires both her ugly
and pretty roots,
savors only off of ripened fruits.

- *The truth leaves mixed berry stains on everything I adore.*

Blue-Red (Bonus)

I saw mints of hue in the sky
with tints of blue that when I cry;
my wail from today to tomorrow
turns pale to gray with such sorrow,
and my veins would reveal
dry stains of teal.

As I heal
through the teal,
and I pray
through the gray;
Blue
would become my view.

I was indeed afraid of being dead
that when I bleed a shade of red;
my heart from dawn to night
breaks apart and has gone white,
and my blood will soon
become a flood of maroon.

...

As I shred the maroon
at noon,
and spread the white
with light;
Red
will become my dread.

- *Blue is the color in which our sorrows turn pale, a hue that loses its pigment when tears start to fall. Teal is the healer, like the sea; Its current drifting us to the shore. Red is the tint where our blood gushes out, leaving a maroon-stained pool when cut. The truth about blue and red, is that they both bring life and death; like our veins, and like our hearts.*

Up

If we weren't afraid of heights
We'd climb the tallest tree
While our thoughts run free
Around the treetop lights.

We'd swing from branch to branch
Reaching the stars
Ignoring the scars
Careful not to fall like an avalanche.

There will be no such thing as fear
The higher we go
The more we will know
Up towards the atmosphere.

- *Do not try and cut down trees, because their goal is to reach for the stars in the sky. With each branch stretching for a wish to hold.*

Facts Vs. Fiction

Truth in her dress,
finds facts too tight.
In fiction,
she slips in lies with ease.

- *She knew the truth couldn't be eased into, so she unmasked it quickly, like ripping off clothes.*

Release

Every single seed
that becomes a tree of life,
must break through
their comfort shell,
to begin growth.

- *Just like us, we must crawl out of our comfort zone to experience the duration of life.*

Yesterday, Today & Tomorrow

The journey to our truths
starts off with too many lies
that's how we live
yesterday's pain
with today's cries
that will become tomorrow's joy.

- *We must go through distances today, to feel close tomorrow. Sweat and tears is worth the fight to our destination, because that's how we know we've tried.*

Branching Out

Even when their branches are bare,
I would still hold hands with the trees.
Trees still feel loved,
when they are abandoned by their leaves.

Still, I stand by trees whose limbs branch out like bones.

- *Branch out from what holds you back.*

The Truth

We wander along
as we stumble upon,
the truth we remembered
the lies that begun.

We never pushed away the lies
until the truth reflect the skies,
it was always there
right in front of our eyes.

- *We seem to realize the truth, after believing all the lies and we will never know the truth before knowing what is truly false.*

Limbs

Dead limbs
reach beyond heaven skies.

- *Even the trees have more faith than you.*

Truth & Lies

Truth, holds steady in spite
of our twisted lies.
Lies, similar to cobwebs;
Ongoing and spinning,
until the truth comes and untangles them.

- *Truth is a dependable light for guidance, while lies lead into dangerous darkness.*

*"The trees spoke up with truths,
that we found ourselves searching for every chance to listen."*

Trees & Truths, a poetry collection that will guide us to exist in the presence of nature (knowing trees), and to become who we truly are with self-acceptance (finding truths). Both the knowledge on trees and the discovery on truths (while we dive into *Trees & Truths*), will bring forth the concept of growth, that will allow us to see what it means to seek self-assurance when surrounded by nature and/or society.

About the Author

Anntonette Jackson is a Canadian Author, emerging Poet and continuing Writer. She was born and raised in Winnipeg, Manitoba, with an ethnic background of Jamaican. She started writing poetry at the beginning of her adulthood, starting off with written love poems then progressively tilting her poetry mainly towards Nature. She expresses her vision through the uses of Personification and Imagery within her writing.

The day the trees begin to speak,
will be the day we learn their truths.

Like two branches of the same tree growing in opposite directions, both our lies and truths experience the same core, but spin and weave differently.

Just as a tree will grow thick scars to protect itself when its trunk or limbs are wounded, we too must discard the lies that ripples us from knowing our truths.

Only if mankind knew how to accept and speak the truth, the world would have become a better place to breathe in.